EMBOUCHURE BUILDER

for

TRUMPET

(Cornet)

for daily use with any method

by

LOWELL LITTLE

Alfred Music
P.O. Box 10003
Van Nuys, CA 91410-0003
alfred.com

ISBN-10: 0-7692-2306-0
ISBN-13: 978-0-7692-2306-3

INTRODUCTION

Two of the most valued qualifications possessed by the successful cornet or trumpet player are flexibility or elasticity of the lips and the ability to support a free-flowing, sonorous tone with the breath in all registers. It is through the development of these qualities only that endurance (the ability to play for long periods of time without undue fatigue) and a pleasing, musical sound may be achieved.

A free and flexible upper register can be developed only through the development of A COMPLETELY RELAXED LOW AND MIDDLE REGISTER!

The great majority of instruction books on the market today neglect the low register almost completely and take the student into his upper register long before he has learned to support his tones properly with his breath. This can result only in excessive mouthpiece pressure, excessive strain, and a forced and inaccurate tone placement. The ability to play except for short periods without fatigue and bruising abuse to the lips, sometimes beyond repair, becomes impossible.

THERE ARE ABSOLUTELY NO SHORTCUTS TO FLEXIBILITY AND ENDURANCE!!

These qualities can be achieved only through diligent, daily, concentrated, practice toward developing a relaxed physical attitude, free from force or strain. Many misguided students are encouraged to use shallow cupped, cushion-rim mouthpieces as a shortcut to endurance and high register. However, the tremendous sacrifice in tone quality and unmusical results generally can never achieve the desired results.

THE PURPOSE OF THIS BOOK

This book has been designed as a supplimentary study to be used along with any standard instruction book. The studies contained herein are excellent for use in the warm-up period prior to each daily session of practice. The technicality of the fingerings is comparatively simple and the studies can be used to advantage by a young student with only a few weeks of formal study. This book contains much valuable material essential to successful performance not found within standard instructional material.

The advanced student will also find much of value in helping him to keep his embouchure and breath support in "tip-top" condition. Many of the exercises can be memorized and utilized as short warm-up drills prior to group rehearsals or public performances. Just as an athlete would never think of entering into a strenuous sport before warming up and limbering up his muscles neither would a true musician think of immediately beginning to play the high register of his instrument or play forte passages without a period of preparation.

SUGGESTIONS FOR THE USE OF THIS BOOK

When practicing sit or stand in an erect but relaxed position. The entire body, including the hands, arms, shoulders, neck, and face, should assume an attitude of physical comfort free from any feeling of anxiety or strain. This cannot be emphasized too strongly!

While the exercises contained here are to be practiced slurred as marked, they can also be played with legato, detached, or staccato tonguing for the advantage of additional dexterity after they have been mastered by slurring.

BREATHING

Breathe naturally but deeply through both the corners of the mouth and the nose. Do not raise the shoulders or allow them to become rigid. Practice holding the lungs full of air with the throat and mouth open before taking up your instrument. Never hold the air in the lungs by closing the throat. Then, try placing the hands over the waist and abdominal area and pronounce the word "hut", with some force, holding the "t". Note how the mid-section and abdominal muscles contract against the hands. This is the natural manner in which these muscles should contract when expelling the air from the lungs into the instrument. The amount of contraction will, of course, increase with the volume desired or the amount of speed required by the column of air passing through the lips to sustain a given pitch. The student must learn through application the exact amount of contraction needed at any given time. Many students find it helpful to wear a wide canvas belt around the waist when practicing until automatic habits are established.

THE EMBOUCHURE

Tone can be produced only by setting the column of air within the instrument into vibration in sympathy with the elastic vibration of the lips. This flexibility can be developed only through the gradual development of the lips by giving them ample opportunity to become accustomed to vibrating without force or strain. Forcing the lips into a vibrating position through excessive mouthpiece pressure can only result in stiffening the vibrating area or in causing irreparable damage to the lip tissues. Many brass players use too much muscular contraction and mouthpiece pressure in the middle register leaving nothing for the higher tones. Complete relaxation of the lips must be achieved in the low register before it becomes possible to produce tones freely in the middle and upper registers. Then, the lips should only be contracted the amount necessary as the pitch ascends.

Never stretch the lips into a smiling position as this tends to weaken the muscles in the vibrating area. Roll the red part of the lips slightly inward in order that the vibrating area may be developed near the lip line where the greater strength and elasticity lies. Keep the corners fo the mouth comparatively loose in order that the lips may be contracted toward the center in ascending pitches. The more rapid vibrations are achieved through the muscular thickening of the vibrating area.

Since the lower lip is more capable of muscular development it is wise to allow the majority of what mouthpiece pressure is necessary to rest on the muscular pad formed by the lower lip in order to protect the more elastic or upper lip. The lips should be kept in constant motion (contracting and relaxing) as you play ascending and descending tonal lines. The lips tire more quickly when held in a rigid, stationary, position and will stay fresh longer if they are kept in motion whereby the blood can circulate through them freely. A high degree of coordination must be developed between the contraction of the lips and the contraction of the muscles of the blowing mechanism.

IN ORDER TO USE THIS BOOK MOST EFFECTIVELY THE STUDENT SHOULD NOT PROCEED BEYOND THE POINT WHERE HE CAN PLAY THE EXERCISES EASILY AND WITHOUT STRAIN! HE SHOULD CONSTANTLY REVIEW BACK TO THE EARLY EXERCISES AS HE PROCEEDS!

Allow the lips and the continuous flow of air do the work. Hold mouthpiece pressure to a minimum. Relax corners of the mouth and drop lower jaw slightly for the lower intervals! Keep red part of lips curved slightly inward. Breathe deeply but keep arms, shoulders, neck, and upper body fully relaxed.

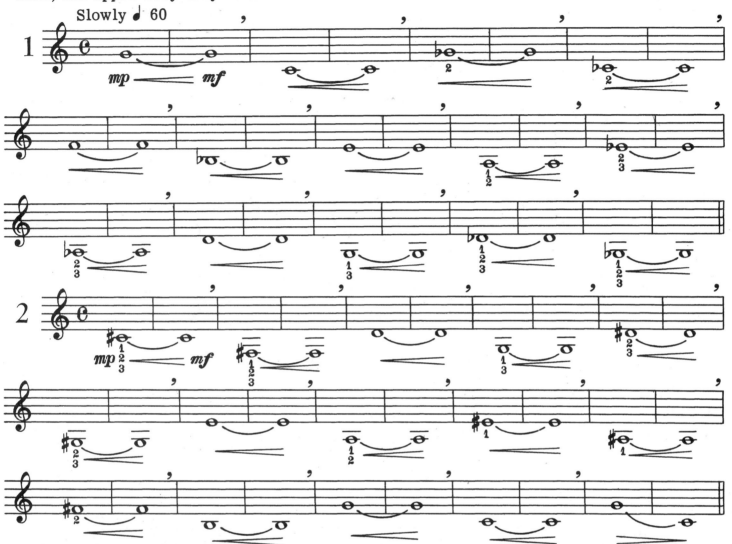

After attack anchor tip of tongue against lower teeth and keep tongue low and well forward. Prepare for drop to lower interval by raising tongue just behind tip to "ee" vowel position on last count of 1st measure. On count one of second measure relax lips, drop lower jaw slightly and return tongue to "ah" vowel position simultaneously.

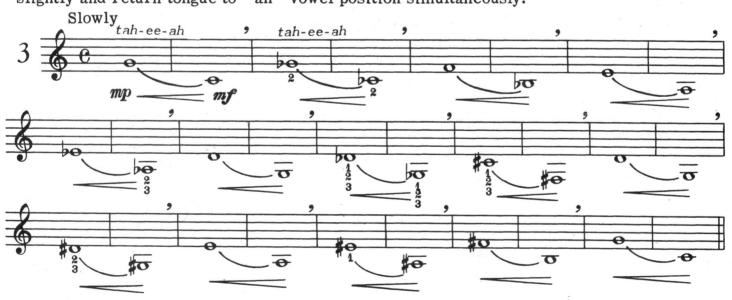

IMPORTANT = Constantly increase volume of air throughout phrase by gradually increasing the contraction of the abdominal muscles. Prepare lips for upward slur on count four of 1st measure. As you execute slur upward raise tongue just behind tip to "ee" vowel position. Return tongue to "ah" position immediately after upper interval is reached. **NEVER ATTEMPT TO FORCE UPWARD INTERVAL!!**

Keep lips in constant motion-contracting upward-relaxing downward.

8

10 Slowly

tahee-ah-eeah-eeah-ah-ah

Do not proceed beyond this page until you are able to play all of the preceding exercises with a free and open tone without force or strain!!!
Repeat 4-8 times. Keep abdominal and lip muscles constantly in motion-contracting and relaxing as you ascend and descend.

11

12

10

Repeat 4-8 times.

Are you able to play everything thus far freely and without strain?

Slowly

tah-eeah-eeah-eeah

Slowly

12

14

When the student has mastered the foregoing exercises, he should be easily able to improvise further exercises based on their principles.